THANKS

RIDDLE

BOOK FOR KIDS

250+ TRICKY RIDDLES & BRAIN TEASERS

BRIGHT MINDS LEARNING

Bright Minds Learning

TABLE OF CONTENTS

INTRODUCTION

Get ready to test your brainpower and tickle your funny bone with the trickiest Thanksgiving riddles around! Whether you're solving these with your family or challenging your friends, this book is stuffed with brain teasers that will keep you thinking and laughing all day long!

Thanksgiving isn't just about the turkey and pie—it's also a time for family, friends, and, of course, fun! This riddle book is your perfect companion to keep everyone entertained, whether you're on a long road trip, waiting for the turkey to finish cooking, or enjoying some after-dinner fun.

The riddles in this book are designed especially for kids like you who love a good challenge. Some will make you think hard, others will have you giggling, and a few might even stump the adults at the table! Don't worry if a riddle seems tough—the real fun is in trying to figure it out. And remember, the more creative you get, the closer you'll be to cracking the code.

So, gather your family, grab some pumpkin pie, and dive into these riddles that will make this Thanksgiving one to remember. Are you ready to get your brain buzzing and your funny bone tickled? Let's get started!

THANKSGIVING BRAIN TEASERS

Before we get into the turkey and stuffing, let's see if you can crack some of the funniest Thanksgiving riddles around!

Do you have what it takes to solve them before dinner is served? Some might seem easy at first, but think twice! They're designed to make your brain work overtime and keep everyone guessing. Let's see if you can rise to the challenge!

Chapter 1 - Questions

Take your time going through the questions. Not every question has an obvious answer—some require careful thinking, while others are just plain silly! As you go through each of these puzzles, don't be afraid to take a wild guess or think outside the box. Whether it's a tricky logic puzzle or a light-hearted riddle, the fun is in the challenge.

1. It's a flower, but it doesn't bloom. It sounds like a month, and it floats on water. **What is it?**

2. I'm a fruit that is tart but paired with sweet. I'm red and small, and at Thanksgiving, I'm a treat. **What am I?**

3. I am something you see each Thanksgiving, but I can also be an emotion. You'll see me on faces, and I'm something you can share. **What am I?**

4. I'm a bird, but you might not want to see me fly. I get stuffed and served, but not in a pie. **What am I?**

5. I'm tall when I'm young, but I shrink as I get older. I bring light to the Thanksgiving table. **What am I?**

Chapter 1 - Questions

6. You can keep me whole or break me apart, either way, I'm important to Thanksgiving tradition. **What am I?**

7. I can be cracked, but I'm not a joke. I'm filled with meat and often eaten as a holiday snack. **What am I?**

8. I'm round, sweet, and sometimes topped with cream. I come after dinner and am part of the Thanksgiving dream. **What am I?**

9. When I'm cooked, I'm soft and creamy. Add gravy to me, and I'm a dream come true, but leave me too long, and I might get lumpy! **What am I?**

10. When the table is set, I'm the dish that never gets touched. I'm passed around, admired, but completely ignored. **What am I?**

11. I'm roasted, stuffed, and carved on Thanksgiving day, but I'm not a turkey. **What am I?**

12. I arrive at the table in a boat but never set sail. **What am I?**

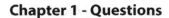

Chapter 1 - Questions

13. I can be mashed, roasted, or baked, but no matter what, I always keep my eyes on you. **What am I?**

14. You can hear me but never see me, and I won't speak unless spoken to. **What am I?**

15. I'm the only thing that makes you stronger the more you take. No, I'm not turkey legs! **What am I?**

16. I can be big and green or tiny and canned, but either way, people always ask, "What am I doing on this plate?" **What am I?**

17. At the start of eternity, at the end of time and space, lies the beginning of the end and the end of every place. **What is it?**

18. If it took 3 men 4 hours to roast a turkey, how long would it take 4 men to roast the same turkey?

19. What do grateful, thankful, wonderful, and joyful have all in common?

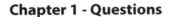

Chapter 1 - Questions

20. How are Thanksgiving and April Fools' Day different?

21. I have ears yet can't hear, and I have drops yet no hair. **What am I?**

22. For what reason did the pilgrims cruise from Britain to America?

23. Why don't turkeys attend Thanksgiving feasts?

24. What has legs but doesn't walk, a body but never moves?

25. You buy me to eat but never eat me. **Who am I?**

26. What starts out cold, ends up hot, and gets gobbled up before you know it?

27. I'm something that everyone can hold, but no one can touch. **What am I?**

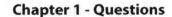

Chapter 1 - Questions

28. What gets dressed every year but never goes anywhere?

29. I get sliced, I get buttered, and sometimes I roll, but I'm never late for dinner. **What am I?**

30. Why do turkeys make good escape artists?

31. Why did the turkey bring a computer to the party?

32. Why did the apple join the circus?

33. What did the cranberry say to the orange at Thanksgiving dinner?

34. Why was the corn so confident?

35. Why do turkeys make terrible comedians?

Chapter 1 - Questions

36

THE TURKEY GLOVE GRAB

Thanksgiving is around the corner, and you're getting ready to help in the kitchen. The problem is, you need a pair of oven mitts, but all the mitts are mixed up in a drawer!

There are 20 red oven mitts and 20 blue oven mitts. It's completely dark, and you can't see the colors. What is the minimum number of mitts you must pull out to ensure that you have at least one matching pair?

37

FARMER JOE'S PUMPKIN PATCH

It's Thanksgiving season, and Farmer Joe needs to plant his pumpkin patch in a special way to make sure there's enough for both pies and decoration.

He has 5 fields available. He wants to plant at least 2 fields with pumpkins and at least 2 fields with corn. How many different ways can he plant his fields?

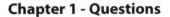

Chapter 1 - Questions

38

TURKEY'S TREASURE TROVE

In a secret part of the barn, there's a stash of 50 golden corn kernels that everyone wants to share before Thanksgiving dinner.

You and your friend take turns picking between 1 and 5 kernels. Whoever takes the last kernel wins. What strategy should you use to ensure that you always win, assuming you go first?

39

GRANDMA'S SECRET THANKSGIVING RECIPE

Grandma has a secret recipe for the best Thanksgiving gravy, but she mixed up the bottles of ingredients! She needs them in the right order to make her famous gravy.

The ingredients are in 5 identical-looking bottles on the kitchen counter. You can only test them one by one, and each time, Grandma will tell you if it's the right one. How can you find the correct sequence with the fewest possible tries?

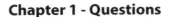

Chapter 1 - Questions

40

THANKSGIVING CANDY MIX

After the big Thanksgiving meal, everyone is ready for some treats. The candy jar has 10 red candies, 12 green candies, and 8 blue candies.

Without looking, you need to pick out enough candies to guarantee you get at least 5 green candies. What is the minimum number of candies you need to pick to be sure you have enough green ones?

41

MAGIC THANKSGIVING MULTIPLES

This Thanksgiving, you notice Grandma's old recipe book has a sequence of magic numbers written in the back. It seems that each number multiplies itself to help calculate servings for the big meal. Can you figure out the next number in this pattern?

The sequence is: 3, 9, 27, ?. What is the next number in the sequence?

Chapter 1 - Questions

42

THE THANKSGIVING RIVER CROSSING

On Thanksgiving morning, a girl needs to cross a small river to gather ingredients for her family's feast. She has her dog, a bag of cranberries, and her turkey. The boat can only carry one item plus the girl at a time. If left alone, the dog will chase the turkey, and the turkey will peck at the cranberries.

How can the girl get all three items across safely without anything being eaten or lost?

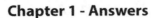

Chapter 1 - Answers

1. The Mayflower.

2. A cranberry.

3. A smile.

4. A turkey.

5. A candle.

6. A wishbone.

7. A nut.

8. Pumpkin pie.

9. Mashed potatoes.

10. The gravy boat.

Chapter 1 - Answers

11. A ham.

12. Gravy.

13. Potatoes.

14. An echo.

15. Steps (like footsteps).

16. Green bean casserole.

17. The letter E.

18. None, the turkey is already roasted.

19. They are all stuffed (full).

20. One is for thanks, the other is for pranks!

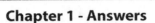

Bright Minds Learning

Chapter 1 - Answers

21. Corn.

22. Since they missed their plane!

23. They're always stuffed!

24. A dining table.

25. A fork.

26. The Thanksgiving turkey.

27. A conversation.

28. A turkey.

29. A dinner roll.

30. Because they always have a wing to get away!

Bright Minds Learning

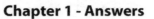

Chapter 1 - Answers

31. To keep track of all the "fowl" play!

32. Because it wanted to be the apple of everyone's eye!

33. "We make a great zest-y pair!"

34. Because it was always "ear-resistible!"

35. Because they always "chicken" out on stage!

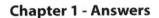

Chapter 1 - Answers

36. The Turkey Glove Grab

To guarantee a matching pair, you need to pull out 3 oven mitts. If you pull out only 2 mitts, you could end up with one red and one blue, which wouldn't match. By picking 3 mitts, you are guaranteed that at least two of them will be the same color.

37. Farmer Joe's Pumpkin Patch

Farmer Joe has 5 fields and wants to plant at least 2 fields with pumpkins and 2 fields with corn. Here are the possible combinations:

- 2 fields with pumpkins and 3 fields with corn

- 3 fields with pumpkins and 2 fields with corn

Since there are different combinations for arranging these fields, there are 6 possible ways in total for Farmer Joe to plant his fields while meeting the requirements.

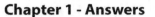

Chapter 1 - Answers

38. Turkey's Treasure Trove

To ensure that you win, you need to use a strategy that leaves your opponent with a multiple of 6 coins after each of your turns.

- Start by picking 2 coins on your first turn, leaving 48 coins.

- After that, pick a number of coins that will leave your opponent with a multiple of 6 each time. For example, if your friend picks 2 coins, you pick 4 coins, and so on.

By always leaving a multiple of 6, you will force your opponent into a position where you are the one to pick the last coin and win.

39. Grandma's Secret Thanksgiving Recipe

To find the correct sequence of potion bottles with the fewest possible tries, use a systematic trial and elimination approach:

- Label the bottles as 1, 2, 3, 4, 5.

- Start by testing a sequence and put them in a row, such as 1, 2, 3, 4, 5.

- Each time Grandma tells you if it's correct or not, put the

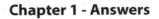

Chapter 1 - Answers

incorrect bottle to the end of the row.

- Continue this process until you determine the correct order.

The trick is to use what you learn from each step to reduce the number of tries, ensuring you are being systematic to minimize the total number of attempts.

40. Thanksgiving Candy Mix

In the worst case scenario, you could pick all of the red and blue candies before getting any green ones.

- There are 10 red candies and 8 blue candies, which is 18 candies in total.

- To make sure you get at least 5 green candies, you would need to pick 5 more candies after the 18, totaling 23 candies.

Therefore, you must pick 23 candies to guarantee you have at least 5 green candies.

Chapter 1 - Answers

---

41. Magic Thanksgiving Multiples

The sequence is 3, 9, 27, ?.

- The pattern is that each number is multiplied by 3.

- After 27, the next number is 27 x 3 = 81.

So, the next number in the sequence is 81.

42. The Thanksgiving River Crossing

To get the dog, the cranberries, and the turkey across the river without anything being eaten:

- First, take the turkey across the river.

- Go back alone and take the dog across.

- Bring the turkey back to the original side.

- Take the cranberries across to the other side.

- Finally, go back and bring the turkey across.

This ensures that the dog and turkey are never left alone together, and the turkey and cranberries are never left alone together, resulting in a safe crossing for all.

GOBBLE, GOBBLE! TURKEY RIDDLES

Thanksgiving wouldn't be the same without turkeys! In this chapter, these feathery friends will challenge your brain with riddles.

Get ready for some tricky fun!

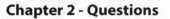

Chapter 2 - Questions

The game is now picking up its steam! Grab a pen and some paper, draw out the scenarios, and see what works. Don't worry if you don't get it right away - the fun starts when you think hard to figure it out.

1. I am light as a feather and easy to lift, but I bet you can't throw me to the turkey!

2. When does Christmas come before Thanksgiving?

3. What can never be eaten at Thanksgiving dinner?

4. What has feathers, bows its head, and kneels as if in prayer?

5. Can a turkey fly higher than an ostrich?

6. Where did pilgrims land when they arrived in America?

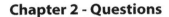

Chapter 2 - Questions

7. What do the Pilgrims, Indians, and Puritans have in common?

8. What smells the best at Thanksgiving dinner?

9. Where do turkeys go to dance?

10. I am a fruit that can be used to sip water. **What am I?**

11. Remove the outside, cook the inside. Eat the outside, throw away the inside. **What am I?**

12. I'm a bell that doesn't jingle, and I sound spicy, but I won't make you sweat. **What am I?**

13. Take off my skin for a Thanksgiving dish—I won't cry, but you will! **What am I?**

14. I'm a room that you can eat. **What am I?**

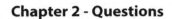

Chapter 2 - Questions

15. I'm a turkey's worst nightmare, but I'm a chef's best friend. **What am I?**

16. What's something you'll always find in the middle of Thanksgiving, even though you can't see it?

17. I'm the first to arrive at Thanksgiving, but the feast can't begin without me. **What am I?**

18. Why don't you like eating fish on Thanksgiving?

19. What's big, colorful, and floats through the streets on Thanksgiving Day but doesn't need any air to breathe?

20. I'm sweet but don't talk, I'm round but don't roll, and I'm baked but not bread. **What am I?**

21. I'm something you look at on Thanksgiving but never watch, I'm thin but cover a lot of space. **What am I?**

22. Why did the family bring a ladder to Thanksgiving dinner?

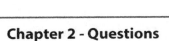

Chapter 2 - Questions

23. What can be served but is never eaten, and if it runs out, the meal might be late?

24. When can you serve something without cooking or eating it?

25. I come in the morning but leave before dinner. You can't eat me, but without me, you might be late for the feast. **What am I?**

26. What's something you'll always find in the center of attention at Thanksgiving dinner, but you can't see it?

27. I wear a coat in the fall but lose it by dinner. **What am I?**

28. Why don't cranberries ever get lonely?

29. I'm not on the menu, but I'm always in the room. I'm never on a plate, but everyone gives thanks for me. **What am I?**

Chapter 2 - Questions

30. What always goes up but never comes down at Thanksgiving?

31. Why did the turkey refuse dessert?

32. How do turkeys send messages?

33. What game do turkeys love to play?

34. Why did the turkey want to be in a band?

35. How do turkeys stay in shape?

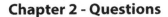

Chapter 2 - Questions

36

THE FEATHER COUNT DILEMMA

Tom and Tina Turkey each have a pile of feathers. They decide to share their feathers equally, but they don't remember how many they each had. The only clue is: when Tom gives 7 feathers to Tina, Tina ends up with double the feathers Tom has left. In total, they have 21 feathers. How many feathers did Tom and Tina originally have?

37

THE ODD HAT OUT

8 turkeys are preparing for Thanksgiving and each wears a hat of one of 4 colors: red, blue, yellow, and green. There are exactly 2 hats of each color. If each turkey can see all other turkeys, can they know what color hat they themselves have?

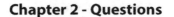

Chapter 2 - Questions

38

TURKEY'S GREETINGS

The turkeys are gathering to discuss how to escape this Thanksgiving. 7 turkeys, each shakes "wings" only once with each of the others, how many wing-shakes will there have been?

39

THE MYSTERY OF THE CORN EARS

Tom the Turkey is in charge of organizing three boxes filled with corn ears, but he lost the tags showing how many ears are in each box. Here's what Tom knows:

- The total number of corn ears in Box 1 and Box 2 is 33.

- The total number of corn ears in Box 2 and Box 3 is 28.

- The total number of corn ears in Box 1 and Box 3 is 31.

Can you help Tom figure out how many corn ears are in each box?

Chapter 2 - Questions

40

TURKEY PARADE ARRANGEMENT

There are 6 turkeys getting ready for the Thanksgiving parade. Each turkey must stand in a row, but Tom cannot stand next to Tina. How many different possible arrangements are there for the 6 turkeys to stand in the parade line?

41

THE TURKEY'S GOLD HUNT

Tom Turkey has discovered a map with a series of numbers leading to a hidden treasure. The numbers are: 2, 6, 12, 20, 30, ?. What is the next number in the sequence, and how is the pattern related to finding the treasure?

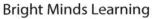

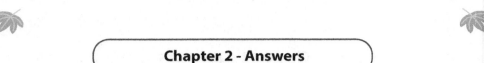

Chapter 2 - Answers

1. A feather.

2. In the dictionary.

3. Thanksgiving breakfast.

4. A praying turkey.

5. Of course. Ostriches don't fly.

6. On their feet.

7. The letter "I".

8. Your nose. Even all year round!

9. The Butter Ball.

10. A strawberry.

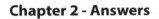

Chapter 2 - Answers

11. Corn.

12. A bell pepper.

13. An onion.

14. A mushroom.

15. An oven.

16. The letter "G".

17. The table.

18. It's because Thanksgiving Day never falls on a Fry-Day.

19. A parade balloon.

20. A pie.

Chapter 2 - Answers

21.   A tablecloth.

22.   Because they heard the mashed potatoes were on another level!

23.   The clock.

24.   When you serve a tennis ball.

25.   The sunrise.

26.   The letter "n" in dinner.

27.   A corn husk.

28.   Because they always come in a bunch.

29.   Family.

30.   Your appetite!

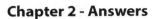

Chapter 2 - Answers

31. It was already stuffed!

32. By "feather-mail!"

33. Duck, duck... turkey!

34. Because it was good at "winging" it!

35. They do lots of "wing-ups"!

Chapter 2 - Answers

36. The Feather Count Dilemma

We know that after Tom gives 7 feathers to Tina, Tina ends up with double the number of feathers that Tom has left, which means Tom has one-third of the total feathers. Therefore, Tom has 7 feathers after giving 7 to Tina.

Originally, Tom had 14 feathers, and Tina had 7 feathers.

37. The Odd Hat Out

The turkeys can determine their hat colors by using logical deduction. They can strategize beforehand as follows:

- Each turkey will count how many hats of each color they see.

- Since there are exactly 2 hats of each color, each turkey knows that if they see 2 hats of a certain color, their hat must be a different color.

- By discussing and confirming the count of each color they see, they can deduce their own hat color.

This way, all 8 turkeys can determine their hat color correctly.

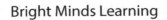

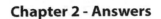

38. Turkey's Greetings

If we number the turkeys from 1 to 7, turkey 1 will shake "wings" with turkeys 2 through 7, turkey 2 will shake "wings" with turkeys 3 through 7 (as it has already shaken wings with turkey 1), and so on.

Total of wing-shakes will be: $6 + 5 + 4 + 3 + 2 + 1 = 21$.

39. The Mystery of the Corn Ears

Let's add the totals of Box 1 and Box 2, Box 2 and Box 3, and Box 1 and Box 3: $33 + 28 + 31 = 92$.

This sum represents twice the total number of corn ears across all three boxes, so the total number of corn ears in all three boxes is 46.

From this, we can find the number of corn ears in each box:

- Box 1: $46 - 28 = 18$ corn ears

- Box 2: $46 - 31 = 15$ corn ears

- Box 3: $46 - 33 = 13$ corn ears

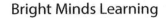
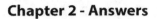

Chapter 2 - Answers

40. Turkey Parade Arrangement

First, calculate the total number of ways to arrange 6 turkeys, which is 720. Then calculate the total of ways to arrange turkeys where Tom stands next to Tina, which is 240.
So the remaining 720 − 240 = 480 is the total number of ways to arrange the turkeys where Tom doesn't stand next to Tina.

41. The Turkey's Gold Hunt

The given sequence is 2, 6, 12, 20, 30, ?. To find the next number in the sequence, notice that the differences between consecutive terms form the sequence 4, 6, 8, 10. The next difference should be 12.

Thus, the next number in the sequence is 42.

PILGRIMS, PUMPKINS, AND PUZZLES

Step back in time with the Pilgrims and early settlers!

This chapter is filled with history, Thanksgiving traditions, and tricky puzzles that will test your holiday knowledge in a fun way.

Let's see if you can solve them before the Pilgrims set sail again!

Chapter 3 - Questions

1. I sailed across the ocean but have no sails. I landed in America but have no feet. **What am I?**

2. Why did the Pilgrims sail on the Mayflower?

3. How can you make an apple stop rolling down a hill?

4. I'm a tiny seed, but I grow into something tall. My golden kernels feed people in the fall. **What am I?**

5. Why did the Pilgrims always win at cards?

6. What did the Pilgrims plant to grow their houses?

7. Why did the Pilgrims throw their bread into the ocean?

8. Why don't turkeys ever get in trouble?

9. What did the pumpkin say to the Pilgrim?

Chapter 3 - Questions

10. I'm round and shiny, but I'm not a coin. I'm part of the first Thanksgiving, but you won't find me on a plate. **What am I?**

11. What do you call a Pilgrim who loves to play sports?

12. Why did the pumpkin become friends with the scarecrow?

13. You reap what you sow because of me. Remove the first three letters, and I become an object you can wear. **What am I?**

14. If the Pilgrims were alive today, what would they be most famous for?

15. April showers bring May flowers. What do May flowers bring?

16. Why do you get lower grades after Thanksgiving?

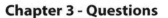

Chapter 3 - Questions

17. I'm tall and dark with a big gold buckle, but if you saw me today I might make you chuckle. **What am I?**

18. Which is heavier: a ton of potatoes or a ton of turkey feathers?

19. What did the broccoli say to the carrot during the race?

20. Which of the Thanksgiving beverages always sounds sad?

21. A cowboy rode into town on Friday. He stayed for three nights and rode out on Friday. How is this possible?

22. I grow underground, but I'm not a mole. I'm baked, mashed, or fried, and I'm always part of the Thanksgiving bowl. **What am I?**

23. Why did the pumpkin sit on the doorstep?

Chapter 3 - Questions

24. What has a neck but no head?

25. What comes down but never goes up?

26. What five-letter word typed in all capital letters can be read the same upside down?

27. Two moms and two daughters are at the Thanksgiving table, yet there are only three people at the table—how is that possible?

28. Why is it easy to talk to a turkey?

29. I am used when cooking but I don't cook. I keep your clothes clean but I don't wash. I hang from your neck but I am not a necklace. **What am I?**

30. I have feathers but no wings. I can fly. My sting can be deadly. **What am I?**

Chapter 3 - Questions

31. Why are giblets always doing crazy things?

32. Why did the Pilgrim sit on a pumpkin?

33. What did the Pilgrim do when it couldn't find its belt?

34. Why did the Pilgrims always bring extra socks?

35. Why do pumpkins make the best storytellers?

Chapter 3 - Questions

36

THE PILGRIM'S CORN RATION PUZZLE

The Pilgrims have 100 ears of corn to share among 5 families, but each family must get a different amount of corn, and no family can get 0 ears. How can the Pilgrims divide the 100 ears of corn so that all the conditions are satisfied?

37

THE PILGRIMS' FRUIT BASKET

The Pilgrims are preparing for the Thanksgiving feast, and they brought 5 baskets filled with fruit. Among these, there are 2 baskets of apples and 3 baskets of oranges. The number of fruits in each of the 5 baskets are as follows: 60, 45, 75, 65, 55.

It is not known which baskets contain apples and which contain oranges, but it is known that the total number of oranges is double the total number of apples. Can you figure out which baskets contain oranges?

Chapter 3 - Questions

38

THE PILGRIM'S FOOT RACE

During the Thanksgiving feast, 5 Pilgrims decide to have a foot race. The Pilgrims are Peter, Mary, John, Sarah, and Tom. Peter finished ahead of Mary but behind John. Sarah finished behind Tom but ahead of Peter. John finished ahead of Tom. Who finished in second place?

39

THE PILGRIM'S PET

Tom the Pilgrim has a pet squirrel named Nutty, and Nutty wants to climb to the top of a tall tree that is 10 meters high. Every day, Nutty manages to climb up 4 meters, but every night, Nutty slips down 3 meters while resting. If Nutty starts climbing on a Monday morning, which day will Nutty finally reach the top of the tree?

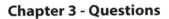

Chapter 3 - Questions

40

THE HARVEST

Every day, Tom the Pilgrim helps gather apples from the orchard. To leave the orchard, Tom has to pass through 4 baskets, and at each basket, he must leave behind half of the apples he has. At the end of the day, Tom manages to bring 10 apples home. How many apples did Tom originally have before placing any in the baskets?

41

THE PILGRIM'S FAMILY

There is a Pilgrim family with 3 sons. Each son has one older sister and one younger sister.
Can you guess how many children are in this Pilgrim family in total?

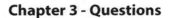

42

THE THANKSGIVING RIVER CROSSING PUZZLE

A Pilgrim family needs to gather firewood across a river for their campfire. The family includes a mother, a father and two sons. Both the mother and father weigh 70 kg, while each son weighs 35 kg. However, the boat can only carry a maximum of 70 kg. How can the whole family cross the river safely?

43

THE THANKSGIVING MARKET

To prepare for Thanksgiving feast, a Pilgrim went to the market to buy a turkey for $60. He then sold the turkey for $70, making a profit. Later, he regretted selling it, so he bought it back for $80. Finally, he sold the turkey again for $90. How much profit did the Pilgrim make in total?

Chapter 3 - Answers

1. The Mayflower.

2. Because there weren't enough seats on the turkey!

3. Put it in a pie dish.

4. Corn.

5. Because they had a lot of "hearts"!

6. A roof garden!

7. To make sure it didn't go "stale" on the journey!

8. Because they can talk their way out of a "jam!"

9. "I'm not your average squash!"

10. A harvest moon.

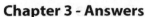

Chapter 3 - Answers

11.   A ball-grim!

12.   They both had great "field" experience!

13.   Har-vest.

14.   Their age.

15.   Pilgrims.

16.   Because everything is always marked down after the holidays.

17.   A pilgrim hat.

18.   Neither, because they both weigh a ton.

19.   "I'm rooting for you!"

20.   Apple sigh-der.

Chapter 3 - Answers

21. His horse's name is Friday.

22. A potato.

23. Because it was waiting to be picked!

24. A bottle.

25. Rain.

26. SWIMS.

27. They are a grandma, mom, and daughter.

28. Because they're always gobbling up the conversation!

29. An apron.

30. An arrow.

Chapter 3 - Answers

31. Because they're a little offal!

32. Because it wanted to have a gourd time!

33. It used a piece of "rope-gourd!"

34. To have a "pair-a-docks" for every situation!

35. They're full of "plot twists!"

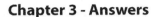

> **Chapter 3 - Answers**

36. The Pilgrim's Corn Ration Puzzle

There are many ways to divide the 100 ears of corn to 5 families. One possible solution is:

- Family 1: 10 ears

- Family 2: 15 ears

- Family 3: 20 ears

- Family 4: 25 ears

- Family 5: 30 ears

This way, all conditions are satisfied: each family gets a different number of ears, and the total is 100 ears of corn.

37. The Pilgrims' Fruit Basket

The total number of oranges is double the total number of apples. Therefore, the sum of all the fruits (apples and oranges) must be three times the total number of apples.
Total number of apples: $(60 + 45 + 75 + 65 + 55) : 3 = 100$ apples.

It is easy to see that the baskets containing 45 and 55 fruits must be the ones with apples, since they add up to 100.

Thus, the two baskets with 45 and 55 fruits contain the apples, while the other three baskets contain the oranges.

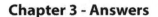

Chapter 3 - Answers

38. The Pilgrim's Foot Race

From the clues, we can deduce the order of finishing as follows:

1. John

2. Tom

3. Sarah

4. Peter

5. Mary

Therefore, Tom finished in second place.

39. The Pilgrim's Pet

Nutty the squirrel will take 6 days to reach a height of 6 meters. Every day, Nutty climbs 4 meters but slips down 3 meters at night, making a net gain of 1 meter per day.

After 6 days, Nutty reaches 6 meters. On Sunday afternoon, Nutty makes the final 4-meter climb to reach the top of the tree without slipping back down. Therefore, Nutty will reach the top on Sunday.

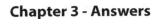

Chapter 3 - Answers

40. The Harvest

The total number of apples that Tom originally gathered:
$10 \times 2 \times 2 \times 2 \times 2 = 160$ apples.

The number of apples left in the 4 baskets is 150 apples.

41. The Pilgrim's Family

The family must have one daughter, who is the eldest, so that all three sons have an older sister.

The family must also have another daughter, who is the youngest, so that all three sons have a younger sister.

Therefore, the family has a total of 5 children.

42. The Thanksgiving River Crossing Puzzle

To solve this puzzle, the family needs to use a strategy that involves multiple crossings with different family members. Here's the step-by-step solution:

- First Trip: The two sons (35 kg each) cross the river together. Now both sons are on the other side, while the parents are still on the original side.

- Second Trip: One son takes the boat back across the river.

Chapter 3 - Answers

Now one son is back on the original side with the parents.

- Third Trip: The father crosses the river alone. Now the father is on the other side, and one son is there too.

- Fourth Trip: The remaining son on the other side takes the boat back to the original side.

- Fifth Trip: The two sons cross the river again together. Now the two sons and the father are on the other side.

- Sixth Trip: One of the sons takes the boat back across the river.

- Seventh Trip: The mother crosses the river alone.

- Eighth Trip: The son who took the boat back earlier finally returns to the other side.

Now the entire family is safely across the river, and they can proceed to gather firewood for their campfire.

43. The Thanksgiving Market

The Pilgrim made a profit of $10 each time he sold the turkey, resulting in a total profit of $20.

FEAST OF FUN RIDDLES

Food is always fun! This chapter is full of riddles about tasty treats.

From fruits to veggies, see if you can solve these food-themed puzzles before your next meal!

Chapter 4 - Questions

1. How can you drop a raw egg onto a concrete floor without cracking it?

2. What do you call a bear with no teeth?

3. I'm something that's better when I'm cracked, especially at breakfast. **What am I?**

4. I make a loud sound when I'm changing. When I do change, I get bigger but weigh less. **What am I?**

5. I'm orange, wear a green hat, and even though I sound like a parrot, I won't repeat what you say. **What am I?**

6. What do you call an angry carrot?

7. What did the tomato say to the other tomato during a race?

8. I'm something that gets dressed up in layers, but you'll never see me at a fashion show. **What am I?**

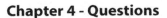

Chapter 4 - Questions

9. A butcher is five feet ten inches tall and wears size 13 shoes. What does he weigh?

10. What kind of cup doesn't hold water?

11. I wear a red coat and have a stone inside. **What am I?**

12. I'm a fruit with a crown on top, and my house is tough to crack. **What am I?**

13. Sometimes I'm light, sometimes I'm dark, but I always melt in your mouth. **What am I?**

14. What do you get from a pampered cow?

15. What do you call a cow with no legs?

16. I'm a house for two, sometimes one. Break my walls, eat the inside, and throw me away. **What am I?**

17. What did the baby corn say to the mama corn?

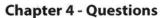

Chapter 4 - Questions

18. What did the nut say when it sneezed?

19. I'm made from my mother. I hang until I'm half gone, then sleep in a cave until I'm ready. **What am I?**

20. How do chickens bake cakes?

21. What did the mayonnaise say when someone opened the refrigerator door?

22. Where do tough chickens come from?

23. Why do beets always win?

24. What do you call a bagel that can fly?

25. What vegetable is the most fun and always invited to parties?

26. What do you call it when a baby chicken takes a bathroom break?

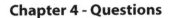

Chapter 4 - Questions

27. What did the doctor prescribe to the sick lemon?

28. I am a bird, I am a fruit and I am a person. **What am I?**

29. Which fruit is a celebrity?

30. What is the longest fruit?

31. What question can you never answer yes to?

32. How far can a fox run into a grove?

33. When it comes to me, you go on red and stop on green. **What am I?**

34. What do you call a dog that sweats so much?

35. A container holding water but not a cup. If you want to find me, look up. **What am I?**

36

THE PUMPKIN PATCH

Tom and his family visited a pumpkin patch to pick out the perfect pumpkins for Thanksgiving. There are 8 pumpkins in the patch, and all of them look the same, but one is slightly heavier than the rest. With only two weighings on a balance scale, how can Tom figure out which pumpkin is the heaviest?

37

THE THANKSGIVING FRUIT BASKET PUZZLE

There are three baskets at the Thanksgiving feast. One basket contains only apples, one contains only pumpkins, and one contains both apples and pumpkins. However, each basket has been labeled incorrectly - meaning none of the labels match the actual contents. By opening just one basket and picking out one piece of fruit without looking inside, how can you determine the correct labels for all three baskets?

Chapter 4 - Questions

38

APPLE SHARING

You have 20 delicious apples in a basket at Thanksgiving gathering. 20 children come up to you, each asking for an apple. You want to share the apples with all the children but keep one apple in the basket. How can you do that?

39

VEGETABLE MEDLEY

There are 4 types of vegetables on the table: carrots, peas, corn, and potatoes. If there are 3 more peas than carrots, 2 fewer corns than peas, and the same number of potatoes as carrots, how many of each vegetable are there if the total count is 24 vegetables?

Chapter 4 - Questions

40

THE THANKSGIVING PIE MYSTERY

The Pilgrim family returned home to find their favorite pumpkin pie smashed on the kitchen floor.

They immediately questioned the 4 turkeys living nearby, who responded as follows:

Tom Turkey: "It wasn't Tina. It was Dale."

Tina Turkey: "It wasn't Chuck. It wasn't Dale."

Chuck Turkey: "It wasn't Dale. It was Tina."

Dale Turkey: "It was Chuck. It was Tina."

It is known that each of them told one true statement and one false statement. Who smashed the pie?

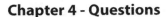

Chapter 4 - Questions

41

THE THANKSGIVING COIN CHALLENGE

You are blindfolded and 10 coins are placed in front of you on the table. And you are allowed to touch the coins but can't tell which way up they are by feel. You are told that there are 5 coins head up, and 5 coins tail up but not which ones are which. Can you make two piles of coins each with the same number of heads up? You can flip the coins any number of times.

42

THE LIGHTING PROBLEM

Your family goes to Uncle Joe's house to celebrate Thanksgiving. It's getting dark and Uncle Joe tells you to turn on the light in the dining room. However, the light switch is in the next room. When you go to the next room, you find 3 light switches. All the lights are currently off, and you can only enter the dining room once. How can you determine which switch controls the dining room light?

Chapter 4 - Questions

43

THE THANKSGIVING TAX TRICK

During Thanksgiving, a famous tax collector set up a checkpoint with strict rules:

Anyone bringing livestock through the checkpoint must give up half of their animals. If the number of animals is odd, they must give up half plus half an animal. After that, the collector returns 1 animal to the owner.

Three Pilgrim brothers are bringing 5 turkeys across the checkpoint. Knowing the rules, the eldest brother comes up with a clever plan so that they don't lose any turkeys.

How did they manage to cross without losing a single turkey?

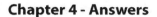

Chapter 4 - Answers

1. Concrete floors are very hard to crack.

2. A gummy bear.

3. An egg.

4. Popcorn.

5. A carrot.

6. A steamed veggie.

7. "Ketchup."

8. A sandwich.

9. Meat.

10. Cupcake.

Chapter 4 - Answers

11. A cherry.

12. A pineapple.

13. Chocolate.

14. Spoiled milk.

15. Ground beef.

16. A peanut.

17. "Where's pop?"

18. "Cashew!"

19. Cheese.

20. From scratch.

Chapter 4 - Answers

21. "Close the door, I'm dressing!"

22. Hard-boiled eggs!

23. They are un-beet-able.

24. A plane bagel.

25. A fungi (fun guy)!

26. Chickpeas!

27. Lemon-aid.

28. Kiwi.

29. Star Fruit.

30. Longan.

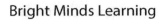

Chapter 4 - Answers

31. "Are you asleep?"

32. Only halfway—then he's running out of it!

33. A watermelon.

34. Hot dog.

35. Coconut.

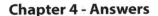

Chapter 4 - Answers

36. The Pumpkin Patch

First, take 6 of the 8 pumpkins and split them into two groups of 3, placing each group on either side of the balance scale. Leave the remaining 2 pumpkins aside.

If the scale balances, that means the heaviest pumpkin is one of the 2 pumpkins left out. Simply weigh those 2 pumpkins against each other to find out which one is heavier.

If the scale doesn't balance, then the heaviest pumpkin is in the heavier group of 3. In this case, take 2 of those 3 pumpkins and place them on either side of the scale. If they balance, the heaviest is the one that wasn't weighed. If they don't balance, the side that goes down contains the heaviest pumpkin.

37. The Thanksgiving Fruit Basket Puzzle

First, open the basket labeled "Apples and Pumpkins" and take out one piece of fruit. Since the labels are all incorrect, the basket you opened must contain only apples or only pumpkins. Let's say the fruit you took out is an apple. This means that the basket labeled "Apples and Pumpkins" only contains apples.

Next, the basket labeled "Pumpkins" cannot contain only pumpkins, nor can it contain only apples since the labels are incorrect. Therefore, it must contain both apples and pumpkins. The last basket, labeled "Apples," must then contain only

73

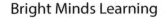

Chapter 4 - Answers

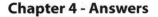

pumpkins.

This way, you can correctly label all three baskets.

38. Apple Sharing

Give 19 apples to 19 children. Then, hand the basket with the final apple to the last child. This way, everyone gets an apple, and you still have one apple in the basket!

39. Vegetable Medley

Carrots: 5

Peas: 8

Corn: 6

Potatoes: 5

40. The Thanksgiving Pie Mystery

Since one of Tina's statements is true, the culprit must be either Chuck or Dale. Since one of Dale's statements is true, the culprit must be either Chuck or Tina. The intersection leads to Chuck.

Tom and Chuck, whose statements are logically identical, both indicate that Chuck is the culprit, each making one true

Chapter 4 - Answers

statement ("It wasn't Dale") and one false statement ("It was Tina"). Thus, all their replies are consistent with Chuck being the one who smashed the pie.

41. The Thanksgiving Coin Challenge

First, divide the 10 coins into two groups, each containing 5 coins. Then, take one of the piles and flip all the coins in that pile. This way you successfully created two piles with the same number of heads!

42. The Lighting Problem

First, turn on switch 1 and leave it on for a few minutes.

Then, turn off switch 1 and quickly turn on switch 2. Now, enter the dining room to check the light.

If the light is on, then it is controlled by switch 2.

If the light is off, feel the bulb. If the bulb feels warm, then it is controlled by switch 1, since it was left on for a while before being turned off. If it feels cold, then it is controlled by switch 3, as it was never turned on.

This way, you can correctly determine which switch controls the dining room light!

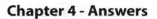

Chapter 4 - Answers

43. The Thanksgiving Tax Trick

The brothers decided to split the turkeys among themselves, each taking 1 or 2 turkeys through the checkpoint individually. By doing this, each brother was able to avoid losing any turkeys, and they successfully crossed without any loss!

FAMILY TIME RIDDLES

Thanksgiving is about more than just food—it's also about family!

This chapter is full of riddles that celebrate family traditions, gatherings, and the silly moments we all experience during the holidays.

Chapter 5 - Questions

1. What do you get when you cross a turkey with a comedian?

2. Why did Grandma bring a ruler to Thanksgiving dinner?

3. What's something that always makes the rounds at Thanksgiving but never stays in one place?

4. How do you organize a space themed party with your family?

5. Your dad and his boss have the same parents but are not siblings. How is this possible?

6. What's the best way to get everyone's attention at the Thanksgiving table?

7. Why did the pie get in trouble at the family dinner?

Chapter 5 - Questions

8. I'm something everyone in the family shares, but it's not a dish. **What am I?**

9. Why was the Thanksgiving dinner so noisy?

10. What do you call the family member who always tells jokes at Thanksgiving?

11. Why did the mashed potatoes join the band?

12. What happens when everyone at Thanksgiving tries to tell their story at the same time?

13. Which family member always gets picked on at Thanksgiving?

14. Why did the cranberry sauce bring an umbrella to dinner?

15. Why was the stuffing invited to every family dinner?

Chapter 5 - Questions

16. What's a family's favorite type of music on Thanksgiving?

17. Inside a huge palace on a desert island there were a king, queen, and twins – but no people. How can that be?

18. What did the gravy say when it got poured over the turkey?

19. Why did the fork and spoon start arguing?

20. What do you call it when the family cat jumps on the table during dinner?

21. What did Grandpa say when the turkey started telling jokes?

22. Grandpa went for a walk, and it started raining. He forgot to bring an umbrella and didn't have a hat. When he got home, his clothes were soaking wet, but not a hair on his head was wet. How was this possible?

Chapter 5 - Questions

23. What do you call it when the family falls asleep after dinner?

24. I am your mother's brother's only brother in law. **Who am I?**

25. What's a sure way to know the turkey has had enough of the family gathering?

26. I am a mother and father, but never birth or nurse. I'm rarely still, but I never wander. **What am I?**

27. If six children and two dogs were under an umbrella, how come none of them got wet?

28. Why did the apple pie break up with the pumpkin pie?

29. Why did the mashed potatoes get invited to all the parties?

Chapter 5 - Questions

30. Why did the turkey bring a microphone to Thanksgiving dinner?

31. What is the longest word in the dictionary?

32. You see a boat filled with people. It has not sunk. But when you look back, you don't see a single person on the boat. Why?

33. What can be touched but can't be seen?

34. What can go through glass without breaking it?

35. What do you call a sad cup of coffee?

Chapter 5 - Questions

36

TURKEY IN DISGUISE

There are five individuals, consisting of 4 real Pilgrims and 1 turkey in disguise.

Only one of them is lying, and the rest always tell the truth.

The 1st Pilgrim says, "I am a real Pilgrim."

The 2nd Pilgrim says, "I am the turkey in disguise."

The 3rd Pilgrim says, "The first Pilgrim is lying, and the second Pilgrim is truthful."

The 4th Pilgrim says, "One of us is not a real Pilgrim."

The 5th Pilgrim says, "The first Pilgrim is a real Pilgrim."

Who is the turkey?

Chapter 5 - Questions

37

THE HOLIDAY TRADITION SHUFFLE

The Pilgrims follow a specific tradition for the Harvest Festival. On the first day, they sing a song; on the second day, they light a lantern; on the third day, they bake bread. If this pattern continues, what will they do on the seventh day?

38

TURKEY'S ESCAPE PLAN

The turkey and the hunter met by the river. The hunter wanted to catch the turkey and said:

"I will ask you 50 questions. You must answer all of them with just one response, or I'll catch you!"

The turkey agreed.

The hunter then asked 50 questions rapidly, covering all sorts of topics. He was certain he would capture the turkey this time. However, to his surprise, the turkey gave just one answer that covered all the hunter's questions.

What is the answer?

Chapter 5 - Questions

39

THANKSGIVING CUP CHALLENGE

At the Thanksgiving dinner table, there are 7 cups that are all facing up. Each turn, you can change the position of 3 cups—either flip them to up if they are down or down if they are up. The goal is to have all the cups facing down.

How many steps will it take to turn all the cups down?

40

THANKSGIVING TRADITION RIDDLE

Every Thanksgiving, the Pilgrims have a tradition of lighting candles. The first year they lit one candle, the second year, they lit three, and the third year, they lit six. How many candles will they light in the fifth year?

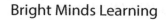
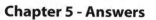

Chapter 5 - Answers

1. A bird that can crack you up!

2. To make sure everyone measured up!

3. The bread basket.

4. You planet.

5. He's self-employed.

6. Say, "I think I just saw the turkey move!"

7. Because it was too flaky!

8. A laugh.

9. Because it was stuffed with chatter!

10. The pun-kin!

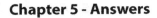

Chapter 5 - Answers

11. They wanted to get in on the "mash-up!"

12. A "corn-fusion!"

13. The turkey—it always gets roasted!

14. In case there was a food fight!

15. Because it was always full of good ideas!

16. Plymouth Rock!

17. They are mattresses.

18. "Looks like we're in this together!"

19. Because the knife was trying to stir things up!

20. A cat-astrophe!

Chapter 5 - Answers

21. "Now that's some fowl humor!"

22. He is bald.

23. A "nap-kin" gathering!

24. Your dad.

25. It starts giving everyone the cold shoulder!

26. A tree.

27. Because it wasn't raining.

28. Because it found someone sweeter!

29. Because they know how to mash things up!

30. To give a 'winged' performance!

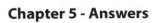

Chapter 5 - Answers

31.   Smiles, because there is a mile between each 's'.

32.   All the people on board are married.

33.   Your heart.

34.   Light.

35.   Depresso.

Chapter 5 - Answers

36. Turkey in Disguise

If the 3rd Pilgrim were telling the truth, it would mean that the 2nd Pilgrim is the turkey, and the 1st Pilgrim is lying. However, this contradicts the information that there is only one liar. Therefore, the 3rd Pilgrim must be the liar. If the 3rd Pilgrim is lying, the 2nd Pilgrim is telling the truth, so he is the turkey in disguise.

37. The Holiday Tradition Shuffle

To solve this puzzle, we need to identify the pattern in the sequence of activities the Pilgrims follow.

- First day: Sing a song

- Second day: Light a lantern

- Third day: Bake bread

The pattern repeats every three days. Thus, on the seventh day, the Pilgrims will sing a song, as the sequence starts over again.

38. Turkey's Escape Plan

The turkey said: "I don't know."

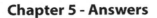

Chapter 5 - Answers

39. Thanksgiving Cup Challenge

It takes 3 steps:

- First Step: Flip any 3 cups down.

- Second Step: Flip 2 down cups and 1 up cup.

- Third Step: Flip the remaining 3 up cups to face down.

40. Thanksgiving Tradition Riddle

Let's determine the differences between each year's candles: between first and second year is 2 candles and between second and third year is 3 candles.

The differences suggest that each year, the number of candles increases by an incrementally larger value than the previous year.

Continuing this pattern:

- Fourth year: Add 4 more candles than the third year to light 10 candles.

- Fifth year: Add 5 more candles than the fourth year to light 15 candles.

Hi there, Amazing Reader!

Thank you for joining us in having a lot of fun puzzles, brain-teasers and laughters for this Thanksgiving!

If you had as much fun reading as we did creating it, we'd love to hear your thoughts.

Reviews help other readers discover the book and let us know what you enjoyed the most. Whether it's a tricky puzzle, a corny joke or just the overall experience, your feedback means the world to us.

So, if you have a moment, please leave a review and share the Thanksgiving fun with others!

Scan this QR Code to leave a review!

To thank you, there are some bonuses waiting for you.

Simply scan this QR Code to unlock them!

AFTER-FEAST BRAIN TEASERS

You've eaten too much, and now it's time to sit back and relax—but wait! Your brain still needs a workout.

These post-feast brain teasers are here to keep you thinking even when you're feeling stuffed!

Chapter 6 - Questions

1. What gets wetter as it dries?

2. The more you take, the more you leave behind. **What are they?**

3. I have roots nobody sees, I am taller than trees. I never grow but I tower. **What am I?**

4. If you have me, you want to share me. If you share me, you no longer have me. **What am I?**

5. What has keys but can't open locks?

6. I am not alive, but I grow. I don't have lungs, but I need air. **What am I?**

7. The more you take away, the larger I become. **What am I?**

8. What has a face and two hands but no arms or legs?

Chapter 6 - Questions

9. What runs but never walks, has a bed but never sleeps, and has a mouth but never talks?

10. I am always hungry and will die if not fed, but whatever I touch will soon turn red. **What am I?**

11. What has an eye but cannot see?

12. What word is spelled wrong in every dictionary?

13. What has one head, one foot, and four legs?

14. I am full of holes, but I can hold water. **What am I?**

15. What has cities but no houses, forests but no trees, and rivers but no water?

16. If two's company and three's a crowd, what are four and five?

17. What can travel around the world while staying in a corner?

Chapter 6 - Questions

18. The more you have of it, the less you see. **What is it?**

19. What begins with T, ends with T, and has T in it?

20. What has an endless supply of keys but no door to unlock?

21. I am light as a feather, yet the strongest man cannot hold me for much longer than a minute. **What am I?**

22. What has fingers but no bones?

23. What has a heart that doesn't beat?

24. If you drop me, I'm sure to crack, but give me a smile, and I'll always smile back. What am I?

25. What is always in front of you but can't be seen?

26. What has 4 eyes but can't see?

Chapter 6 - Questions

27.   I shave every day, but my beard stays the same. **What am I?**

28.   What begins with an "e" and only contains one letter?

29.   I have keys that open no locks, I have space, but I don't have room, you can enter, but you can't go outside. **What am I?**

30.   What can fill a room but take up no space?

31.   What gets sharper the more you use it?

32.   What starts with gas and has three letters?

33.   If you say my name, I no longer exist. **What am I?**

34.   When we stand it lies flat. When we lie back it stands up. **What is it?**

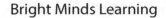

Chapter 6 - Questions

35

THANKSGIVING WEEK MYSTERY

One day, Tom the Pilgrim is walking through the woods and wants to know what day of the week it is. He comes across a turkey and a squirrel and decides to ask them.

The turkey lies ONLY on Monday, Tuesday, and Wednesday. The squirrel lies ONLY on Thursday, Friday, and Saturday.

The turkey says, "Well, yesterday was one of my lying days."

Since Tom can't figure it out just from the turkey's answer, he asks the squirrel. The squirrel says, "Yesterday was also one of my lying days."

What day is it?

36

GRANDPA'S OLD RECIPE BOOK

Grandpa has an old recipe book with 120 pages, but some pages have been lost over the years. The missing pages are 18, 32, 81, and 105.

How many pages are left in Grandpa's book?

Chapter 6 - Questions

37

THANKSGIVING COOKING CHALLENGE

Emily visits her grandmother during Thanksgiving preparations. Grandma has five glass bowls on the table, each containing a clear liquid: cooking wine, saltwater, vinegar, sugar water, and hot water. Grandma smiles and challenges Emily:

"You can only try each once. Can you figure out which bowl holds which ingredient?"

38

THANKSGIVING CHESS CHALLENGE

During Thanksgiving, I played chess with two of my brilliant friends, and both defeated me easily. A young cousin of mine, who is only 10 years old and just learning to play, confidently said, "I can play against both of them at the same time and do better than you—I won't lose to both!"

How could my cousin succeed?

Chapter 6 - Questions

39

THE MISSING COIN MYSTERY

During Thanksgiving, Emma borrows $50 from her mom and $50 from her dad to buy a special pie for the family, which costs $97. She has $3 left, and decides to give $1 back to her mom, $1 back to her dad, and keeps $1 for herself.

Now, Emma thinks: "I owe $49 to my mom and $49 to my dad, which totals $98, and I still have $1. Where did the missing $1 go?"

40

THE THANKSGIVING WATER CHALLENGE

During Thanksgiving preparations, the family has a barrel of water and two jugs: one can hold 5 liters, and the other can hold 7 liters. The goal is to measure exactly 4 liters of water.

Can you help them out?

Bright Minds Learning

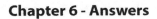

Chapter 6 - Answers

1.   A towel.

2.   Footsteps.

3.   A mountain.

4.   A secret.

5.   A piano.

6.   Fire.

7.   A hole.

8.   A clock.

9.   A river.

10.   Fire.

Chapter 6 - Answers

11. A needle.

12. Wrong.

13. A bed.

14. A sponge.

15. A map.

16. Nine.

17. A stamp.

18. Darkness.

19. A teapot.

20. A music sheet.

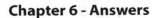

Chapter 6 - Answers

21. Your breath.

22. A glove.

23. An artichoke.

24. A mirror.

25. The future.

26. Mississippi.

27. A barber.

28. An envelope.

29. A keyboard.

30. Light.

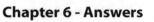

Chapter 6 - Answers

31. Your brain.

32. A car.

33. Silence.

34. Foot.

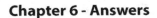

Chapter 6 - Answers

35. Thanksgiving Week Mystery

If today is one of the turkey's "truth-telling" days, it must be Thursday, as this is the only truth-telling day preceded by a lying day. If today is one of the turkey's "lying" days, it must be Monday, as this is the only lying day preceded by a truth-telling day.

Thus, from the turkey's response, Tom knows that today is either Thursday or Monday.

If today is one of the squirrel's "truth-telling" days, it must be Sunday. If today is one of the squirrel's "lying" days, it must be Thursday.

For both the turkey's and squirrel's statements to be consistent, Tom must conclude that today is Thursday.

36. Grandpa's Old Recipe Book

If page 18 is missing, it means page 17 is also lost. If page 32 is missing, page 31 is gone too, and so on.

So, a total of 8 pages are missing.

Therefore, the number of pages left in the book is 112 pages.

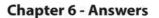

Chapter 6 - Answers

37. Thanksgiving Cooking Challenge

- Touch to find hot water.

- Smell to identify the vinegar and cooking wine.

- Taste to distinguish the saltwater from the sugar water.

38. Thanksgiving Chess Challenge

The secret lies in copying one player's moves and using them against the other. My cousin would make the exact move of my first friend when playing against my second friend, and vice versa. This strategy ensures that if one player wins, the other will lose, meaning my cousin can't lose both games.

39. The Missing Coin Mystery

The confusion comes from incorrectly adding the $1 Emma kept to her total debt. The correct way to think of it is that she owes $98 in total ($49 to each parent), and she also has a $97 pie and $1 in cash. Therefore, $97 (pie) + $1 (cash) equals the $98 she owes her parents. There is no missing dollar - it's just a matter of mixing up the calculations.

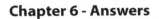

Chapter 6 - Answers

40. The Thanksgiving Water Challenge

• Fill the 7-liter jug to the top and pour water into the 5-liter jug until it's full.

• Now, there are 2 liters left in the 7-liter jug.

• Empty the 5-liter jug completely and transfer the 2 liters from the 7-liter jug into the 5-liter jug.

• Fill the 7-liter jug again and use it to top off the 5-liter jug, which already has 2 liters in it. Since the 5-liter jug needs 3 more liters to be full, you will have exactly 4 liters left in the 7-liter jug.

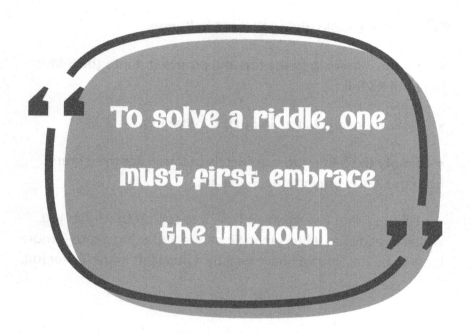

To solve a riddle, one must first embrace the unknown.

Anonymous

SILLY & TRICKY RIDDLES

Sometimes, the best riddles are the ones that make you laugh!

This chapter is all about fun riddles that will keep you giggling with friends and family long after the Thanksgiving leftovers are gone.

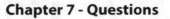

Chapter 7 - Questions

1. Why did the scarecrow win an award?

2. What kind of key opens a banana?

3. Why are ghosts bad at lying?

4. What kind of tree fits in your hand?

5. Why did the bicycle fall over?

6. Why did the bear bring a suitcase to the party?

7. Why don't skeletons fight each other?

8. What did one plate say to the other?

9. Why was the math book sad?

10. What do you get if you cross a snowman and a dog?

Chapter 7 - Questions

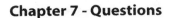

11. Why did the golfer bring two pairs of pants?

12. What do you call a sleeping bull?

13. Why did the carrot get embarrassed?

14. What do you call a fish with no eyes?

15. Why did the music teacher need a ladder?

16. What do you call an alligator in a vest?

17. Why was Cinderella so bad at soccer?

18. What do you get when you put three ducks in a box?

19. Why did the cookie go to the doctor?

20. What kind of music do mummies listen to?

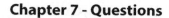

Chapter 7 - Questions

21. Why was the computer cold?

22. What do you call a dinosaur with an extensive vocabulary?

23. Why did the student eat his homework?

24. Why did the cat sit on the computer?

25. What do you call fake spaghetti?

26. Why did the picture go to jail?

27. What has four wheels and flies?

28. Why did the turkey learn to play the drums?

29. What did one ocean say to the other ocean?

30. Why do seagulls fly over the sea?

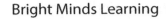

Chapter 7 - Questions

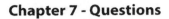

31.   Why was the broom late?

32.   What do you call a lazy kangaroo?

33.   Why are frogs so happy?

34.   What do you call a cow that plays an instrument?

35.   Why did the tomato go to the party alone?

36.   Why did the football team go to the bank?

37.   Why did the belt get arrested?

38.   What do you call a bee that's having a bad hair day?

Bright Minds Learning

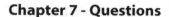

Chapter 7 - Questions

39

THE THANKSGIVING MAZE TRICK

During the Thanksgiving festivities, a turkey is exploring a maze. It takes the turkey an hour and a half to waddle clockwise around the maze. When waddling counterclockwise, it also takes the turkey ninety minutes.

Why is there a difference?

40

THE THANKSGIVING WATER PUZZLE

For the Thanksgiving feast, you need to measure exactly 4 liters of water, but you only have two jugs: one holds 3 liters, and the other holds 5 liters. How can you do it?

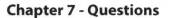

Chapter 7 - Questions

41

THE FARMER'S MIXED EGG SALES

A farmer brings two baskets to the market, each containing 30 eggs. Originally, she planned to sell the eggs at 1 coin for 3 eggs from one basket and 1 coin for 2 eggs from the other basket. However, she decides to sell a mix of eggs at 2 coins for 5 eggs. Does this change benefit the farmer compared to the original plan?

42

THE TURKEY EGG PROBLEM

There are four turkeys in the coop. The first turkey lays one egg per day, The second lays one egg every 3 days, The third lays one egg every 4 days, The fourth lays one egg every 7 days.

One day, Mary collects 4 eggs from the coop.

What is the shortest number of days it takes for Mary to collect exactly 4 eggs?

Chapter 7 - Questions

43

THE THANKSGIVING FAMILY REUNION PUZZLE

Three brothers—Pier, Paul, and Jack—gather with their families for Thanksgiving. An old friend joins the reunion and wants to know which child belongs to which brother. After asking the children, he gets the following responses:

Isabella: "I am 3 years older than Sean."

Teresa: "My father is Jack."

Ethan: "I am 2 years younger than Isabella."

Mary: "I prefer playing with my cousins rather than with my brother."

Karen: "I am the daughter of Pier."

Anna: "It's best to play with Uncle Jack's sons."

Sean: "My father and uncles all have fewer than 4 children each."

Nick: "My father has fewer children than any of my uncles."

Which child belongs to which brother?

Chapter 7 - Answers

1. Because he was outstanding in his field!

2. A monkey!

3. Because you can see right through them!

4. A palm tree.

5. Because it was two-tired!

6. Because it heard there was going to be a "pawsome" adventure!

7. They don't have the guts.

8. "Lunch is on me!"

9. Because it had too many problems.

10. Frostbite.

Chapter 7 - Answers

11. In case he got a hole in one.

12. A bulldozer.

13. Because it couldn't stop peeling!

14. Fsh.

15. To reach the high notes.

16. An investigator.

17. She kept running away from the ball.

18. A box of quackers.

19. Because it felt crumby.

20. Wrap music.

Chapter 7 - Answers

21. Because it left its Windows open.

22. A thesaurus.

23. Because his teacher said it was a piece of cake.

24. To keep an eye on the mouse.

25. An impasta.

26. Because it was framed.

27. A garbage truck.

28. Because it wanted to beat the holiday blues!

29. Nothing, they just waved.

30. Because if they flew over the bay, they'd be bagels!

Chapter 7 - Answers

31. It swept in.

32. A pouch potato.

33. Because they eat whatever bugs them.

34. A moo-sician.

35. Because it couldn't find a date.

36. To get their quarterback.

37. Because it was holding up a pair of pants.

38. A frizz-bee.

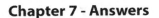

Chapter 7 - Answers

39. The Thanksgiving Maze Trick

There is no difference. An hour and a half are the same as ninety minutes!

40. The Thanksgiving Water Puzzle

First, fill the 3-liter jug to the top and pour it into the 5-liter jug.

Then, fill the 3-liter jug again and use it to fill the 5-liter jug to the top.

Now, there will be 1 liter of water left in the 3-liter jug.

Empty the 5-liter jug completely and pour the remaining 1 liter from the 3-liter jug into the 5-liter jug.

Finally, fill the 3-liter jug to the top and pour it into the 5-liter jug.

You now have exactly 4 liters of water in the 5-liter jug, ready for the Thanksgiving feast!

41. The Farmer's Mixed Egg Sales

Under the original plan, the farmer would earn 10 coins from basket 1 and 15 coins from basket 2, totaling 25 coins.

With the mixed plan, the farmer would earn 24 coins in total.

Therefore, with the mixed plan, he would make less than with

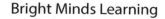
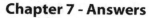

Chapter 7 - Answers

the original one.

42. The Turkey Egg Problem

Let's calculate the number of eggs laid each day.

Day 1: The first turkey lays 1 egg.
Total eggs: 1 egg.

Day 2: The first turkey lays 1 egg.
Total eggs: 2 eggs.

Day 3: The first turkey lays 1 egg, and the second turkey lays 1 egg (since it lays every 3 days).
Total eggs: 4 eggs.

The shortest number of days it takes for Mary to collect exactly 4 eggs is 3 days.

43. The Thanksgiving Family Reunion Puzzle

Let's assume the genders based on the names as follows:
The boys are Ethan, Sean, and Nick.
The girls are Isabella, Teresa, Mary, Karen, and Anna.

Teresa's father is Jack. Anna said Jack has at least 2 sons, and Sean said all the fathers have fewer than 4 children each. So Jack has 3 children.

Chapter 7 - Answers

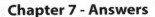

Nick said his father has fewer children than any of his uncles. These clues indicate that Nick cannot be Jack's child. Therefore, Jack's children are Teresa, Ethan, and Sean.

Karen is Pier's daughter. If Mary is also Pier's daughter, then Pier must have a son, who is Nick. But Nick said his father has fewer children than any of his uncles, so Nick and Mary cannot be Pier's children.

Therefore, they must be Paul's children, and Paul only has 2 children.

Pier's children are Karen, Isabella, and Anna.

CONCLUSION

As you sit down for Thanksgiving dinner or share stories with your friends and family, we hope these puzzles remind you of the joy of being curious, trying new things, and working through challenges together. Whether you've solved each puzzle by yourself or as a team, you've shown that there's always more than one way to approach a problem—and that the journey can be just as rewarding as the answer.

If you enjoyed this journey, why not keep the fun going?

Discover more awesome books from Bright Minds Learning that will spark your imagination and keep the fun going.

Scan the QR code below or search Bright Minds Learning on Amazon to explore our full collection and find your next adventure!

Made in United States
Orlando, FL
21 November 2024

54257612R00068